J

The Math of
Hockey

Ian F. Mahaney

PowerKiDS
press

New York

For Brenda

Published in 2012 by The Rosen Publishing Group, Inc.
29 East 21st Street, New York, NY 10010

First Edition

Editor: Joanne Randolph
Layout Design: Greg Tucker

Photo Credits: Cover Dave Sandford/Getty Images for NHLI; p. 4 (bottom) Don Smith/NHLI via Getty Images; pp. 4–5, 10 (left) Bruce Bennett/Getty Images; pp. 6–7, 8, 13 (right) Shutterstock.com; pp. 8–9 Jonathan Daniel/Getty Images; pp. 10–11, 14 (left) Bill Wippert/NHLI via Getty Images; pp. 12–13 Len Redkoles/NHLI via Getty Images; pp. 14–15 Rich Lam/Getty Images; p. 16 Getty Images/NHLI; p. 17 Ken Levine/Getty Images; pp. 18–19 Jed Jacobsohn/Getty Images; p. 20 (left) Al Bello/Getty Images; pp. 20–21 Bill Smith/NHLI via Getty Images.

Library of Congress Cataloging-in-Publication Data

Mahaney, Ian F.
 The math of hockey / by Ian F. Mahaney. — 1st ed.
    p. cm. — (Sports math)
 Includes index.
 ISBN 978-1-4488-2556-1 (library binding) — ISBN 978-1-4488-2698-8 (pbk.) —
ISBN 978-1-4488-2699-5 (6-pack)
 1. Hockey—Mathematics—Juvenile literature. 2. Arithmetic—Juvenile literature. I. Title.
 GV847.25.M333 2012
 796.9620151—dc22
                                    2010029649
Manufactured in the United States of America

CPSIA Compliance Information: Batch #WW11PK: For Further Information contact Rosen Publishing, New York, New York at 1-800-237-9932

Contents

How Does Hockey Work?   4

How Does the Rink Measure Up?   6

The Lines   8

Time   10

What's Your Angle?   12

Penalties   14

What Are the Stats?   16

The Standings   18

The Play-offs   20

Figure It Out: The Answers   22

Glossary   23

Index   24

Web Sites   24

How Does Hockey Work?

Hockey is a sport played on ice skates. Two teams use hockey sticks to try to hit a puck into a goal. The puck is a rubber **disk** 1 inch (2.5 cm) tall and 3 inches (8 cm) across. A goal is scored when one player hits the puck into the

It's a Fact!

The game begins with a face-off. A **referee** drops the puck between two opposing players. The players then try to get control of the puck with their sticks.

net of the other team. The team with the most goals at the end of the game wins.

The team that has the puck is the **offense**. It is trying to score. The other team is the **defense** and tries to stop the offense. Your math skills can help you learn more about this fast-moving game!

Figure It Out!

The offense slaps the puck 50 feet (15 m). The defense then takes the puck away and hits it 70 feet (21 m). How far has the puck moved?

(See page 22 for the answers.)

Each team can have five players and a goalie on the ice.

How Does the Rink Measure Up?

Hockey games are played on an ice rink. In the National Hockey **League** (NHL), a **professional** league, the hockey rink is 200 feet (61 m) long and 85 feet (26 m) wide. The corners of the rink are curved. The curves allow a puck to keep sliding from one wall to the next.

At each end of the rink is a goal with a net. The goal is 6 feet (2 m) wide and 4 feet (1 m) tall. Each team defends one of the goals. The player whose job it is to keep pucks out of his team's goal is called the goalie.

The goals sit in the blue areas at each end of the rink.

Hockey games played in the Olympics and those played in the NHL use rinks of different sizes. Olympic rinks are 60 meters (197 feet) long and 30 meters (98 feet) wide. How much wider is an Olympic rink than the size used in the NHL?

A) 200 − 60 = 140

B) 85 − 30 = 55

C) 98 − 85 = 13

(See page 22 for the answers.)

The Lines

There are many lines painted on the ice rink that tell the players where they are. There is a solid red line 11 feet (3 m) from each end of the rink. These are goal lines. The front of the goal is set in the middle of each line.

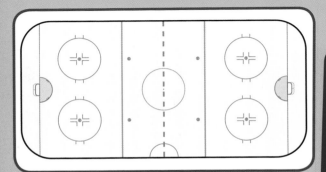

It's a Fact!

There is a dashed red line splitting the rink in two. This is the center line. The face-off opening the game happens in the middle of this line.

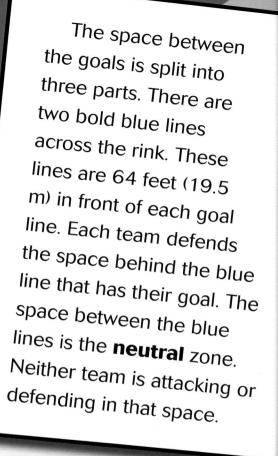

The space between the goals is split into three parts. There are two bold blue lines across the rink. These lines are 64 feet (19.5 m) in front of each goal line. Each team defends the space behind the blue line that has their goal. The space between the blue lines is the **neutral** zone. Neither team is attacking or defending in that space.

This player is just crossing the blue line to leave the neutral zone.

Figure It Out!

Remember that a hockey rink is 200 feet long. Each goal line is 11 feet from the end of the rink. The blue lines are 64 feet from the goal lines. How many feet long is the neutral zone?

(See page 22 for the answers.)

Time

A hockey game is broken into three parts, called periods. In the NHL, a period lasts 20 minutes. Do you want to find out how long a whole hockey game is? You can use math to find out. Your **equation** would look like this:

The scoreboard at a rink tells fans how much time is left in a period. Can you see what period it is and how much time is left here?

20 minutes + 20 minutes + 20 minutes = 60 minutes. Here is another way to say this:

20 minutes x 3 periods = 60 minutes.

Between each period there is a break. The players rest, and coaches plan for the next period.

When a game is tied after three periods, a 5-minute overtime period is played. If the game is still tied, the teams begin a shoot-out.

Here the goalie for the Buffalo Sabres is making a save during a shoot-out against the Montreal Canadiens.

Figure It Out!

In NHL play-off games, teams play in overtime periods until one team wins. The New York Islanders and the Buffalo Sabres play in a play-off game that is tied after three periods. They then play two overtime periods. How long have the teams been playing hockey?

(See page 22 for the answers.)

What's Your Angle?

The space right in front of the goalie is called the slot. When a player shoots on the goal from the slot, she can see a lot of the goal. When a player attacks from the side, he cannot see as much of the goal.

This Chicago Blackhawks player is shooting from the side.

An angle describes a hockey player's point of view. If you have a wide angle in hockey, it means you can see a lot. If you have a narrow angle, you cannot see as much. When a hockey player has a wide angle, it is easier to score a goal.

Figure It Out!

Take a look at these two angles. Which one shows a wide angle, and which shows a narrow angle?

(See page 22 for the answers.)

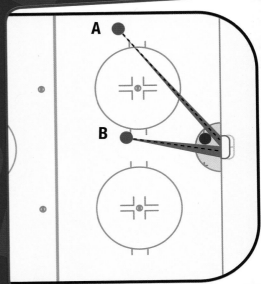

A

B

Penalties

Hockey games can be fast moving and rough. Players often get pushed into the sides of the rink as other players try to steal the puck. Hockey leagues have rules that make games fair and keep players safe. **Penalties** are given out when players break the rules.

This Boston Bruins player is being sent into the penalty box.

It's a Fact!

When one team has more players and they have the puck, it is called a power play.

Figure It Out!

Here Shane O'Brien of the Vancouver Canucks hits Patrick Sharp of the Chicago Blackhawks in the neck with a high stick.

George receives a penalty of 5 minutes for elbowing, or hitting another player with his elbow. What percentage of a 20-minute period is he in the penalty box?

(See page 22 for the answers.)

For example, a player's stick cannot hit another player above the shoulders. This is called high-sticking. When high-sticking happens, the player who did it is given a penalty of 2 minutes. This means she sits in a penalty box for 2 minutes and her team has fewer players on the ice than the other team. This gives the other team a better chance to score a goal.

15

What Are the Stats?

Fans and coaches like to compare players and teams to find out which is the best. When someone studies a group of numbers to understand something better, that person is using **statistics**. A fan can study a player's stats to see how many shots he makes, how often he is in the penalty box, or even how many fights he starts.

Amazing Stats

In his career in the NHL, Wayne Gretzky scored 894 goals and had 1,963 assists. His points total was 894 + 1,963 = 2,857 points. That makes him the NHL career leader in points!

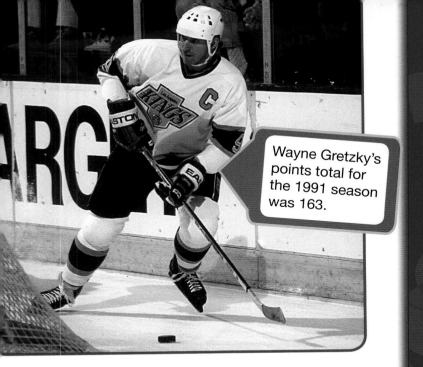

Wayne Gretzky's points total for the 1991 season was 163.

An important statistic for goalies is save percentage. Save percentage is found by dividing the number of saves a goalie makes by the number of shots taken against her. Kim plays goalie. She had 10 shots taken against her and 1 goal was scored. What is her save percentage?

(See page 22 for the answers.)

In the NHL, one of the simpler stats is a player's points. This stat adds a player's numbers of goals and assists. A player scores a goal when he puts the puck in the net. He gets an assist when he passes the puck to a teammate who scores a goal.

The Standings

There are 30 teams in the NHL. These teams are divided into two **conferences**. To find out how many teams are in each conference, you would write: $30 \div 2 = 15$ teams. In each conference, there are three equal **divisions**. How can you find out how many teams each division has? This is the equation to find this answer: $15 \div 3 = 5$. Each division has 5 teams.

The San Jose Sharks and the Detroit Red Wings both play in the Western Conference.

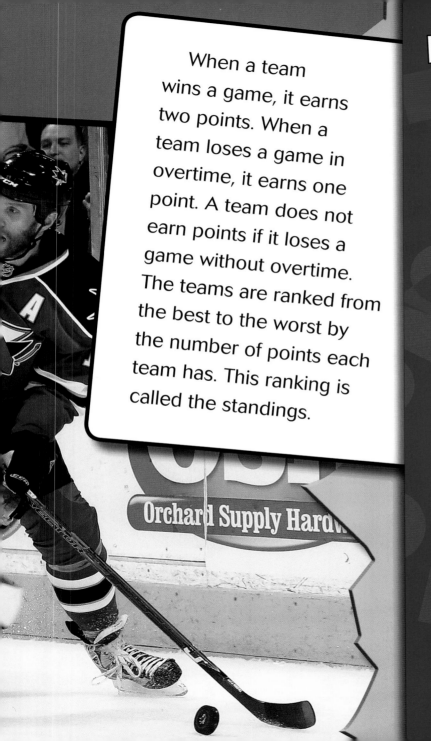

When a team wins a game, it earns two points. When a team loses a game in overtime, it earns one point. A team does not earn points if it loses a game without overtime. The teams are ranked from the best to the worst by the number of points each team has. This ranking is called the standings.

Figure It Out!

If the Detroit Red Wings have 44 wins, 14 overtime losses, and 24 regular losses, how many points does the team have?
A) 44 + 14 + 24 = 82
B) (44 x 2) + 14 = 102
C) (44 x 2) + 14 − 24 = 78

(See page 22 for the answers.)

The Play-offs

Each year, the best 16 teams in the NHL make it into the play-offs. The play-offs are games in which the best teams play each other to find out which team will become the champion.

Jonathan Toews of the Chicago Blackhawks holds up the Stanley Cup after his team won the Stanley Cup Final in 2010.

In the first round of the play-offs, 16 teams play in eight **series** of games. Each series is seven games long. The team that wins moves on to the next round. The team that loses is out of the play-offs.

There are a total of four rounds of play-offs. In each round, half the teams are knocked out.

The last round has two teams and is called the Stanley Cup Final. The team that wins this last series is the NHL's champion.

Brent Seabrook of the Blackhawks fights off Scott Hartnell of the Philadelphia Flyers during the 2010 Stanley Cup Final.

There are 30 teams in the NHL. What is the percentage of NHL teams that make the play-offs?

(See page 22 for the answers.)

Figure It Out: The Answers

Page 5: 50 feet + 70 feet = 120 feet.

Page 7: C). You need to make sure you use the same unit of measurement. This answer uses feet. You can solve this problem using meters, too: 30 meters − 26 meters = 4 meters.

Page 9: The neutral zone = 200 feet − 11 feet − 11 feet − 64 feet − 64 feet = 50 feet.

Page 11: The teams have played hockey for (3 x 20 minutes) + (2 x 5 minutes) = 60 minutes + 10 minutes = 70 minutes.

Page 13: A) is the narrow angle and B) is the wide angle.

Page 15: (5 ÷ 20) x 100 = 25 percent

Page 17: Kim had 9 saves, so her save percentage is 9 ÷ 10 = .900. Save percentages in hockey are expressed with three decimal places. A percentage in other cases is multiplied by 100 and written as 90%.

Page 19: B). The Red Wings have 102 points. Remember you do not count losses in regular games.

Page 21: 53%. How do you find the answer? First, divide the number of teams that make the play-offs by the total number of teams (16 ÷ 30 = .53). Then multiply by 100 to get the percentage (.53 x 100 = 53%).

Glossary

conferences (KON-frens-sez) Groupings of sports teams.

defense (DEE-fents) A team that is trying to stop the other team from scoring.

disk (DISK) An object with a flat, circular shape.

divisions (dih-VIH-zhunz) The smallest groupings of teams in the NHL.

equation (ih-KWAY-zhun) A math statement that says that two different things are equal.

league (LEEG) A group of teams that play one another.

neutral (NOO-trul) Having no one controlling it.

offense (O-fents) A team trying to score points.

penalties (PEH-nul-teez) Punishments for breaking rules.

percentage (per-SENT-ij) One part of 100.

professional (pruh-FESH-nul) Someone who is paid for what he or she does.

referee (reh-fuh-REE) A person who makes sure players follow the rules during a game.

series (SIR-eez) A group of games.

statistics (stuh-TIS-tiks) Facts in the form of numbers.

Index

C
corners, 6
curves, 7

D
defense, 5
disk, 4
division(s), 18

E
equation, 10, 18

F
face-off, 4, 8

G
game(s), 4–8, 10–11,
    14, 19–21

goal(s), 4–5, 7–9,
    12–13, 15–17

I
ice skates, 4

N
National Hockey
    League (NHL), 6–7,
    10, 16–18, 20–21
net, 5, 7, 17

O
offense, 5

P
percentage, 15, 17, 21
player(s), 4, 7–8, 11–17

puck, 4–5, 7, 14, 17

R
referee, 4

S
series, 21
skills, 5
space, 9, 12
sport, 4
stick(s), 4, 15

T
team(s), 4–5, 7, 9, 11,
    14–16, 18–21

W
wall, 7

Web Sites

Due to the changing nature of Internet links, PowerKids Press has developed an online list of Web sites related to the subject of this book. This site is updated regularly. Please use this link to access the list:
www.powerkidslinks.com/sm/hockey/